OLIVES

"From the tree to the table".

By author:
John E. Fecher

ISBN-13:978-1490958057
ISBN-10:1490958053

Self-published

Dedicated to the memory of Aunty Jo (Wilson).

DISCLAIMER/DISCLOSURE:

When you use this book, which is a guideline for curing olives with 100% pure lye crystal drain cleaner, you use it at your own discretion, liability, responsibility and risk. The Author takes no responsibility or liability, etc. for you failing to follow or interpret instructions or safety precautions correctly. Lye is a poison.

I have cured my olives by the method outlined in this book for over fifteen years. I use the lye method. The lye I use is sodium hydroxide, pure 100% crystal lye drain cleaner, sold in the household section of stores. Be aware that you can purchase a "food grade" 100% pure lye from a manufacture over the internet or possibly special order from a hardware store. Please be safe when working with lye, a caustic substance. It is considered a hazardous (volatile) chemical substance. Follow instructions and use lye with care.

This book is intended to be used by adults.

If you feel uncomfortable with using the lye curing method, please find and use a different type of method of curing olives.

This book covers a common method of curing olives with lye. Lye has been used to cure olives by many people, worldwide, for many years. It is also the common method used by big commercial olive producers and "home kitchen" folks. Over the years I have talked to many folks in my area who have olive trees. Many cure small batches of olives each year.

The key to getting the process correct, are the many timed (5 to 8 hour) rinsing's over the 5+ days of curing to get the lye out of the olives.

Index

Introduction

Most my life I have planted trees. When I was a child growing up in Bay Shore, Long Island, New York I would go into the woods and dig up saplings and transplant them on my parents' half acre property. They were mostly apple and maple trees.

Many years later I moved to Northern California. In the early 1990s I bought some land in East Redding to build a house. After moving in I made contact with a fellow who owned a five acre parcel adjacent and behind my property. I purchased that acreage and decided to plant an orchard on it.

The soil was red clay with four to six inch cobbles mixed in. The land had oak and pine trees growing all over it. There was about an acre that had been cleared in the 1940's for a water trough when the area had range cattle on it. The acre was nice, sunny and flat. Now, what type tree to plant on this acre?

In an area southwest of this property, in an area known as Happy Valley, there were hundreds of very old olive trees. I checked out the area. The soil looked like the soil on my property. I stopped and talked to some workers who were picking olives there. The lead man told me the trees were planted eighty to one hundred years ago by a man from Hawaii. He said this would be the last year they would be harvesting these olives. The remaining area of the orchard was being sold by the corporate owner to a land developer for future home sites. He told me this was the last harvest going down south to Corning to be processed. Corning is south of this area by about fifty miles where there are thousands of acres of olives growing. It is known as the "Olive Capital of the World". I knew that olive trees were drought tolerant and could also resist cold in the winter months. So I decided olive trees would be the tree of choice for my orchard. I needed to know where to buy olive trees and how to cure the olives once they produced fruit.

I knew there was an extension of U.C. Davis Division of Agriculture somewhere in the City of Redding, Ca. I located their office and dropped in and explained my problem. This was before the *Internet* was functioning and I needed a real person to ask for the information. They gave me a book request form to mail in to get the University publication 3353* for Olive production. They also told me there were large commercial tree nurseries about one hundred+ miles south in Visalia, Ca. There I could purchase young trees ready for planting. I made that trip to Visalia and bought thirty Manzanillo and eight Ascolano olive trees. These were the type olives said to produce the best table olives.

I had the cleared acre graded (ripped) and marked off, twenty by twenty foot grids. I had a posthole digger come in and sink holes six inches wide by two feet deep. Now there were forty holes ready for planting.

After planting the trees, I ran a drip irrigation system for them, and I was off and running. Picture: **A.**

You do not need to have olive trees to use this book. If you have a tree or two that's great. But maybe your neighbor has trees? You may find some trees planted for landscaping in your town. As long as the trees have not been sprayed with some kind of insecticide or other type chemical, and you have asked permission before picking, you're in business.

If you just want to try my recipe, you can buy a big jar of cured plain olives at a big box store and use them, following my pickled olive recipe instructions.

Olives do not contain acid like other vegetables such as tomatoes. The reason I use vinegar, to pickle the olives, is to add acid to the water to help prevent the formation of bacteria.

Olives would turn to mush if you tried the "canning method" of preservation. I recommend refrigeration of the jars of olives after you finish preparing them and before and after opening the jars. I also recommend labeling them that they "still have pits" in them. You do not want a person cracking a tooth because they are accustomed to pitted olives.

It took five years for me to get a harvest of about three gallons of olives from my trees. I was quite ready to pick and process these olives. At first I used the lye method outlined in the: University of California publication 3353*.

From my experiences over the years, I have modified and expanded on their method. I was going to produce jars of table olives for sale but because of health department rules about processed foods, I only produce jars for friends and relatives. The Ascolano olives are large olives and are better for oil production. They become too mushy for table olives. The Manzanillo olives are perfect. In 2013 I have more olives then I need or can use. I harvest the olives in late September through early November when they just start to ripen on the trees. They **must** be picked when they are ripening but before they change color from green to brownish/ purple. Pictures: **B&C.** If they change color they would only be good for making olive oil. This is because they become too soft for the lye method of curing. I do not make olive oil because special equipment and too much labor is needed for what little is produced.

*Louise Ferguson, G. Steven Sibbett, and George C. Martin. 1994. *Olive Production Manual.* University of California, Division of Agriculture and Natural Resources, Oakland, Ca. Publication 3353. 160pp

Warnings: Lye is a poison! Do not swallow lye, lye solution or lye soaked olives. These could be fatal if swallowed. If swallowed call for emergency help IMMEDIATELY.

READ: WARNINGS, CAUTIONS, ANTIDOTES & FIRST AID ON THE LABLE OF <u>THE LYE CONTAINER</u> BEFORE PROCEEDING!

Be careful not to get lye on your skin. Lye is a Base and it is caustic, and will burn your skin if it is splashed on it. If you do get some on you, spray with 50% water 50% vinegar mixture. The acid mixture will help neutralize the lye. Then rinse with copious amount of water. Picture: J3, M & O2.

Wear a long sleeve shirt to cover skin to protect from splashed lye. Remove any lye splashed clothes and wash skin. Wear eye protection! If lye or lye solution gets in your eyes rinse with copious amounts of warm water. In all these cases see a doctor or get medical attention. Always wear rubber gloves when working with lye. Picture: N. During the curing process keep small children, pets and others away from all the equipment, lye, lye solution and the glass olive jars etc. Always be prudent and keep safety in mind as a top priority! Do not inhale lye fumes.

Pure lye must be used to cure olives in the method used in this book. Pure 100% lye is sold as a drain cleaner/opener. Picture: **M.** It is **sodium hydroxide, 100% pure crystal lye,** and should not have any additives. Always check the lye product, making sure you are using 100% pure lye, without additives or other ingredients. In the 1990s and early 2000's, I could find Red Devil Lye 100% pure lye, sodium hydroxide, (drain cleaner) sold at hardware stores or grocery stores in the cleaners section. As years went by the stores stopped carrying it. You can ask your local hardware store to order a jar of 100% pure crystal lye (sodium hydroxide) for you or you can get it over the internet. Do **not** use a lye drain opener that is **not 100% pure lye** that has additives. (*Never use Drano).* In 2013 I found, sodium hydroxide, pure 100% crystal lye drain cleaner sold at a local chain hardware store I shop.   **Lye is a volatile substance. Add lye to water slowly while stirring. Do not add water to lye, it may react violently (explosively).**

.

Olives are said to be one of the first fruit trees to be planted and cultivated by people. They go back to the beginning of civilization. Olives should be in your diet plan because they are very healthy for you. They make good eating, and a healthy oil too. I use olive oil whenever butter or margarine is called for.

Olives

Equipment needed to cure olives by the pure lye method.

1. **Pure lye:** Use 100% pure crystal lye. I use 100% pure crystal lye (sodium hydroxide, sold as a drain cleaner). Picture: **M**. Lye is a poison if swallowed. If it comes in contact with skin it can burn your skin. If it gets in your eyes it could cause blindness. Keep people, children and animals away from the area where you are curing your olives. After the lye draws the bitterness out of the olives the lye must be completely rinsed (leached) out the olives by soaking in and rinsing with cold water. Picture **M & O2. Note: Plastic containers that come in contact with food or lye should be inert and colorless.**
 2. Large food safe plastic tub. Pictures: **H & I.**

3. Plastic one gallon jar. **Lye safe (inert) will not react to lye.** Picture: **M.**

4. Large stainless steel metal spoon or food grade wood spoon. Never use an aluminum or other type metal spoons, they may react with the lye. Picture: **M.**

5. A "table spoon" measuring spoon. Picture: **M.**

6. Pair of rubber gloves. Picture: **M.**

7. Narrow mouth two gallon Ball jars or food grade, lye safe, plastic equivalent. You can also use well washed **large gallon and ½ gallon** glass or **lye safe/inert** plastic jars from pickles or other food products you can find at restaurants, sandwich shops, or your prior use, etc. "(lye safe means: inert, does not react to or with lye).   Picture: **J, J4, O & O2.**

8. Shaped, steel wire mesh jar cover. Picture: **K.**

9. Scissors. Picture: **L.** Plastic food wrap Picture: **O2.**

10. **Cotton** Cheese cloth. Picture: **L, N & O.**

11. Eye protection (plastic googles or large eye glasses), rubber gloves & a spray bottle containing diluted vinegar/water mixture. Pictures: **J3 & M.**

12. Clean sink. (Example: Deep Laundry sink). Picture: **J3 & O2** If you can leave the jars in the sink while processing is ongoing, it will be safer containing spills.

Curing Olives with Pure Lye Solution.
Narrative

When you pick olives, if some fall to the ground, leave them lay. Use only olives picked from the tree to the basket to prevent contamination from ground bacteria such as fecal matter. Pictures: **D & E.**

After the olives are picked, place them in a large inert plastic food safe tub to be rinsed with cold water. Picture: **I.** Gently stir the olives while rinsing so not to bruise them. Pick out any small, damaged or discolored olives, leaves and twigs. Pour out the water a couple of times until they are well rinsed. You should begin processing olives shortly after picking.

As you can see in Pictures: **J, J2 & J3** when the olives are transferred to the two gallon glass jar, there is a small amount of water in the bottom of the jar. This is to cushion the olives to prevent bruising when dropped into the jar.

I use the two gallon (Ball) glass jar for the curing process. If you cannot find narrow mouth two gallon glass Ball jars you can use jars of other *food safe/lye safe inert* materials. Commercial processing uses large food grade plastic barrels. If you use plastic jars, make sure the plastic will not react with the lye and are food safe, inert and colorless. Good stainless steel spoons are OK. **Never** use anything made of aluminum, copper or other type metals. They may react with lye and poison the olives. The mouth of the jar should be narrow so the olives can be protected from contact with air while curing and rinsing so they do not discolor. Pictures: **N, O & O2.**

Before mixing the lye solution you should prepare a diluted water/vinegar solution (½ water / ½ vinegar), in a spray bottle. This is to spray on and neutralize any lye you may splash on your skin. Wear a long sleeve shirt as protection, remove lye splashed clothes, and always wear rubber gloves when working with lye. Wear eye protection such as large eye glasses or goggles. Should you get lye in your eyes rinse with copious amounts of warm water and **seek emergency treatment by a doctor or emergency medical.** Picture: **M & N.**

I use 100% pure crystal lye (**Sodium Hydroxide**) sold as a drain cleaner. Always check the label on the package to make sure no other ingredients or additives were added to the lye (you need 100% **pure** lye). {*Never use Drano*}. **Always add lye to water (jar will heat up somewhat). Be careful to add slowly and gentle stir when adding lye into water. Never add water to lye. It could become volatile and react explosively.**

As you can see from Pictures: **J3,** I place the two gallon jar in a laundry sink before adding the olives and lye solution. Fill the two gallon jar with rinsed olives to about one and half inches from the top mouth of the jar. Pictures: **J, J2 & J3**.

You will prepare the lye solution in a one gallon lye safe jar. I use an empty lye safe, inert, plastic food jar. Picture: **M.** You may also use a one gallon glass jar. Place this jar in the laundry sink and add one gallon of cold water. In Picture: **M** you see a container of pure 100% crystal Lye, a *table* measuring spoon, a large stainless steel mixing spoon (never use aluminum or other type metal spoons, they may poison the olives) and a one gallon jar to mix the lye in.

"LYE WASH"

The lye wash removes the bitterness from the olives. While stirring with a large stainless steel (or food/lye safe) mixing spoon. Slowly add **four table spoons** of the pure lye to the **cold water** in the **one gallon lye safe inert** jar (jar will heat up slightly). Never add water to lye. It may become volatile and react explosively. Picture: **M.**

Add the olives to the two gallon jar. Picture: **J2.** Leave a one and a half inch space between the olives and the top of the jar. Carefully and slowly pour this lye solution into the two gallon jar that you have filled with olives. Picture: **N.**

Do **not** fill up the one and a half inch space between the top of the jar and the olives. Most likely you will have lye solution left over. Now you will take a hand full of cotton cheese cloth, Picture: **L.** wad it up into a ball and completely fill up the mouth at the top of the jar with the cotton cheese cloth. Picture: **N.**

Take the lye mixing jar, with the left over lye solution, and pour it over the cheese cloth until it is completely and totally saturated to the very top of the jar. Pictures: **N & O.**

Make sure there are no air voids (pockets) in or under the cheese cloth. This is done to keep air from getting to the olives and discoloring them while they cure. If air does get to them the whole batch may be ruined.

Now place plastic food wrap over the mouth of the jar (keeps air from entering the jar) and then the lid. You will now leave the olives stand and soak for **twelve hours** in the lye solution before the next step of the curing process. Picture: **O & O2.** Hopefully you can leave the jars in the laundry sink out of direct sun light and where they are safe from spilling during the process. Some people stir the olives during this process, I do not stir them.

The second Lye Wash.

Twelve hours later: The second lye wash takes place. You will put on your rubber gloves and eye protection etc. and remove the lid and cheese cloth from the olive jar. Place the steel wire mesh cover on top of the jar. Picture: **K.** Tilt the jar over to pour out the lye solution into the laundry sink drain. Take care not to splash lye water on your skin. Right the bottle and fill with fresh cold water rinsing the olives in the wire covered jar. Repeat this rinsing process several times until the brown water run near clear. Rinse out the cheese cloth too.

REPEAT the "LYE WASH" (from page 10).

Yes, now you need to mix the lye solution as before, repeating the previous lye wash process.

After this second **twelve hour** lye wash soak, you will begin the rinsing procedure. If for some reason you let the olives sit in the lye solution a bit longer then twelve hours it will not hurt the process.

Cut into an olive, it should be a **yellow** color down to the pit. If not continue the lye wash. **

Now you must remove all the lye from the olives. You do this by repeated rinsing and letting the olives soak in water. Rinse every 5 to 8 hours, refill jar with fresh cold water and soak for 5 to 8 hours. Repeat this process for 5+ days. The following page describes the rinsing procedure.

** A single page handout titled "ABC's of Home-Cured, Green - Ripe Olives" was my introduction to curing olives with lye (around 1996). The method in this book has modifications from years of curing olives from my trees. The one page handout refers to University of California Cooperate Extension Leaflet 2758. I have recently searched their web-site and U.C. Davis site for this Leaflet and cannot find the actual Leaflet. It may be out of print.

Rinsing Procedure.

You will **repeatedly**, cold water rinse and soak the olives over the next **five+** days. This is to remove (leach out) the lye from the olives. Before you start rinsing and soaking, when you can, cut into an olive and check that it has turned a yellowish color down to the pit. This change from white to a yellowish color indicates that the lye has saturated the olive to the pit.

Put on safety equipment: gloves, eye protection, etc. Remove the jar cover and cheese cloth. Place the wire mesh cover on the jar. Pour out the lye solution and rinse with fresh cold water until the water runs nearly clear. Now fill the jar with clean cold water until the olives are covered. Take the rinsed out cheese cloth and return it to the top of the jar. It should completely cover the olives. If the wad of cheese cloth has shrunk, add more cloth to the wad. Fill the jar with cold water to the very top. Make sure you have saturated the cloth thoroughly getting out all the air pockets. Cover the jar with plastic wrap and the lid. **Picture: O2.**
You will let the jar with fresh water and olives stand for five to eight hours. The lye will begin to leach out of the olives. You will see the water turn brown. Repeat this rinsing/soaking process every **five** to **eight hours for 5+ days.**

Again, remove the cover and cheese cloth. Rinse the cloth and with the wire cover on the jar, drain and the water into the laundry sink. Fill the jar a few times rinsing the olives until the water run clear. Refill the jar with cold water, replace the cheese cloth as before and repeat rinsing/soaking process every to **five to eight** hours. Continue rinsing/soaking process for the next **five+** days. When water is clear, when jar is emptied, the olives are cured and ready. After all these days of rinsing and the water remains clear, you have been successful in curing olives. To check the olives, cut into an olive. The meat of the olive should look white (yellow color gone) down to the pit. If so taste one and it should no longer have a lye taste. It should no longer have a bitter taste. It may have a bland taste. If all these conditions are there you have successfully cured olives! If not continue rinsing procedure.

You must now preserve the olives in a timely manner to prevent bacteria from forming. Olives have very little to no acid content and will quickly spoil. **See: Final Product. Preserving, packing & protecting on page 18.**

.

Curing Olives with pure lye solution.

"Procedure list"
Review all of the proceeding book before using this list!!

1. Put on protective gear. Eye protection and rubber gloves, etc. Prepare water (50%) and vinegar (50%) solution. Picture: **M & J3.** Use this solution if you splash lye onto your skin. Rinse off lye with the water/vinegar solution. Should you splash lye in your eye, rinse with copious amounts of warm water and get medical attention immediately! Should someone swallow lye, lye solution or lye soaked olives, call for emergency help immediately! Call **national poison hotline** if emergency medical doctor or help is not available.

2. Wash your laundry sink really clean or whichever sink you are using. Rinse your olives in big plastic tub and remove leaves and twigs. Picture: **I.**

3. Place two gallon small mouth jars in the sink. I use two gallon glass Ball jars. (see Picture: **J4** for alternatives). Food safe plastic, lye safe, small mouth jars may also work. Pour a small amount of water into the bottom of the jar to buffer the olives as they fall. Gently place olives into the jars until they fill to about an inch and a half from the top of the jars. Pictures: **J, J2.**

4. Prepare the lye solution in a one gallon glass or lye safe plastic jar. Picture: **M.** Fill cold water into the jar. Slowly and carefully add **four** table spoons of 100% pure lye into the water while slowly stirring the solution with the large stainless steel spoon (jar will slightly heat up) (never use aluminum or other types of metal spoon). Lye may become volatile (react explosively) if you mix water into lye.

The lye wash begins.

5. Now slowly pour lye solution into the olive filled two gallon jar to an inch and a half from the top of the jar.

6. Cut and wad up a ball of cheese cloth. Pictures: **L & N.** Place it on top of the olives. Be careful to push down firmly on the cheese cloth to avoid leaving any voids. Now pour in the left over lye solution saturating the cheese cloth and eliminating all air bubbles. Now place a piece of plastic food wrap on mouth of the jar to keep jar air tight. Put the lid back on the jar. Picture: **O & O2.**

7. Let jars with olives and lye solution sit and soak for **twelve hours**. You should keep the jar out of direct sunlight and in a cool environment if possible. It may be best if you can keep the two gallon olive/lye filled jars, while curing, in the laundry sink so they will not be disturbed by children, pets and others.

8. After **twelve hours, put on safety equipment,** remove the lid and cheese cloth and place the steel wire mesh cap over the mouth of the jar. Picture: **K.** Pour out the lye solution. With the wire mesh cover still in place run cold water into the jar. Rinse the olives several times.

The second lye wash!

9. After the last rinse, **repeat step 4, 5 & 6** (The **second** lye wash)

10. Wait for **another twelve hours** of soaking in lye solution.

11. After this total of **twenty four hours** of curing time, the olives should be ready for the rinsing procedure to remove the lye from the olives.

12. Rinse the olives until the water runs clean. Take out an olive and cut it to the pit. It should be a yellowish in color down to the pit. If not, you may want to do another the lye wash for six hours or so.

13 .Now that the lye solution steps are over, you must remove the lye from the olives. **Remember lye is a poison.**

Rinsing procedure

14. RINSE, SOAK, RINSE, SOAK, RINSE, SOAK, RINSE, SOAK, RINSE!.....

15. The rinsing procedure will take **five+ days.** This depends on how often a day you rinse and soak them. Every **five to eight hours** you will remove the cover and place the wire mesh cover on the jar. Pour out the water, rinse out the cheese cloth and rinse the olives until the water runs near clear. Picture: **N.**

16. Then fill with cold water and return the cheese cloth. Remember the cheese cloth must completely cover the olives. Completely saturate the cheese cloth with cold water. You may need to add more cheese cloth to the wad if it has shrunk. Avoid any air bubbles from forming and touching the olives. Place plastic wrap on mouth of jar and then the cover. **Let stand and soak, REPEAT every 5 to 8 hours for next 5+ days.**

17. After all the days of rinsing, water should run clear when emptied. It is time to taste an olive. Cut an olive to the pit, it should be white in color. Bite into one and there should not be any bitter or lye taste. The olives will have a bland taste. If you followed all the instructions you have had success. You must now preserve the olives in a timely manner to prevent bacteria from forming and going bad. Olives have little to no acid in them. Now you are ready to create seasoned pickled gourmet olives. Picture: **T2.** **"Famous Fecher Pickled Olives" If you do not pickle them you must read section: Final Product: preserving, packing, protecting. Page 18.**

Famous Fecher Pickled Olives.
"Recipe ingredients".

1. Liquid mix: one part distilled white vinegar to three parts water. You may use more vinegar but not less.

Following ingredients are for a one quart jar.

2. Lye cured olives.
3. One **Table** spoon of minced garlic.
4. One **Table** spoon of light color Olive oil.
5. Quarter (plus) **Tea** spoon of salt.
6. Quarter Cup of chopped celery.
7. Quarter Cup of chopped onion.
8. Quarter Cup of shredded carrot.
9. Five whole black pepper corns.
10. Ten pickled capers.
11. Other spices are OK but read
    warning: multi spice. Pictures: **R & R3.**

Explanation of ingredients (Pictures: R & R3).

1. **The liquid mix** of one part "white distilled vinegar" to three parts cold water will pickle the olives. The acid of the vinegar will help protect against bacteria forming. Use a one gallon pitcher to mix the vinegar and water. Picture: **S2.** This will make it easier when adding the liquid to the final quart olive jars. Olives contain very little acid. Food acid is added to the mix by pickling them using the acid of the vinegar. This will help to prevent bacteria and mold from forming in the final product. Olives **cannot** be preserved by the canning method. Olives would turn to mush during the hot canning process.

I also strongly recommend the final olives be refrigerated before and after the olives are opened. Jar labels should note "refrigerate" on the labels.

2. I think **Lye cured olives** are the best. There are other ways of curing olives but these other methods are not as effective in getting the bitterness out of the olive. The lye curing method is the only method used in this book. After the olives have been lye cured and well rinsed to eliminate the lye (**see procedure**) they are ready to become "Famous Fecher Pickled Olives".

3. **Minced garlic** can be purchased at local super markets. If you are preparing a great number of jars you can find big containers of the minced garlic for a good price at a superstore. Garlic also will have a preservative effect for olives. Garlic is good for you. Chopped fresh garlic can also be used instead of processed minced garlic.

4. **Olive oil** is added to coat the olives so the added spices and seasoning will cling to the skin of the olives. An inexpensive olive oil is OK to use. It should be light in color.

5. **Salt** should be added in a small amount. I use regular table salt. It is added for flavor and for its preservative properties. Do not use Sea salt or Kosher salts because they vary in strength by measurement. Using too much salt or these salts, may cause the olives to discolor and their skins may shrivel. Nobody wants to eat shriveled up blotchy discolored olives. I use just a Quarter Teaspoon of regular table salt per quart jar. You may use a bit more if you wish.

6, 7 & 8. Use one quarter cup for each of the following: **Chopped white onion, chopped celery and shredded carrot.**

9. Add about eight **whole pepper corns** to each quart jar. This will add a bit of spiciness and give your jars a cool look.

10. Add ten or so **pickled capers** per jar. This will add a zingy taste to the mix. Remember the Super Stores will have the best prices for this type ingredient.

11. **Other** vegetables and spices can be added to your mix. But please read the following warning. Over the years, I have learned from trial and error, some items can be "bad to the taste" when put in the olive jar.

Warning: If you use a **multi spice** and it contains tomatoes or any type of green or hot peppers, these will overwhelm the flavor and perhaps add a bad or bitter taste. Make sure multi seasoning does not contain a lot of salt. Remember too much salt may ruin your olives. If your multi seasoning has salt in the beginning of the list of ingredients, then do not add too much salt (#5).

I sometimes use half a tea spoon of multi seasoning. I always experiment with just a few jars when adding something new to the mix. **You should experiment**. Use other vegetables and seasoning added to the mix. But do not use all your olives up experimenting. If you do not know what the results will be, you may find you will need to be picking and curing more olives!

Very important note!

If you do not use my F.F.P.O. recipe, then some vinegar or another food acid such as: lemon or lime should be included in your finished olives. Olives have very little acid in them. You need to add an acid like these mentioned to help stop bacteria or mold from forming in your finished olives. Please refer to and read section: **Final Product**: **Preserving, Packing, Protecting, Page: 18.**

Final Product.

Preserving, Packing & Protecting.

Safety of your product.

(I wrote this book with the intension that the reader will pickle their olives when the curing process is complete).

This book was written for the purpose of explaining the procedure of curing olives with the traditional lye method. When this process is complete the olives must be protected against the formation of toxic mold and bacteria. This is accomplished by the addition of white vinegar (1 to 3mixture) in the "Famous Fecher Pickled Olive" recipe. This is the method of preserving and protecting the final product. This is accomplished with the acid of white vinegar in the water mixture and the refrigeration of the product at all times.

 Note: I use one quart canning jars for my final product. **Pictures: P, S, T2**. You can reuse jars after they are thoroughly washed. You should always use **new canning jar lids and see that you fill the liquid to the very top of the air tight jar to prevent air pockets.**

Olives are normally picked in October and November. The curing and packing happens as soon as they are picked and washed. The curing and packing should be done in a timely manner. You should not have long delays between steps. This will help prevent contamination of the final product.

continued

Some people finish off the lye curing process by **salt brining** the olives after the olives are completely soaked and rinsed and rid of the lye. Salt brining is done by soaking the olives in a mixture of salt and water (one cup of table salt added to a gallon of water). This solution is then poured over the finished olives, to the very top, protected from air exposure with cheese cloth, and covered and let to stand in a cool place for a 24hrs. Then the solution is poured out and the process repeated for another 24hrs. The olives should absorb some salt to help preserve them. The finished olives are rinsed and then packed in a salt/water solution with some food acid such as vinegar, lemon or lime added to the final jars (then refrigerated).

I **do not** use this method. I did use it when I first started out many years ago when I first began curing olives. You will need to do some testing of your own, adjusting the amount of salt, if the olives become wrinkled or stained. I found the final product did **not** last as long as pickled olives. They were too salty for my taste. One part vinegar three parts water with some salt added was the best for me to finish off (preserve) my olives. People I gave them to, really liked them. They should always be refrigerated.

Remember, the safety of your product is of the utmost concern! "Famous Fecher Pickled Olives", I believe, will best protect against contamination because of the acid of the packing liquids vinegar. They will also have a longer "refrigerator shelf life". My olives are usually finished and packed in late October-early November and handed out to friends and relatives as gifts during the holidays. They then can be used up by the end of the year or beginning of the next year. The user should always smell and visually inspect the olives and jars for spoilage before serving.

Salt Brining Method of **"Curing"** olives is **not** covered in this book.

Picture: **A.**

Olive trees are drip irrigated. These trees are about 18 years old.

Picture: **B.**

Nice large green olives ready for table olive harvest.

Nice green olives, some just beginning to change color (not shown), ready for table olive harvest.

Picture: **C.**

Olives are too ripe for lye curing.

Olives have ripened too much to be table olives. When they begin to turn color as these have, they are only good for making Olive Oil.

Picture: **D.**

To pick the olives, cup your hand around the top of a branch and pull downward toward the end of the branch. The olives will pull off and fall into the plastic container held at the bottom of the branch. Leaves will stay on branch.

Picture: **E.**

John's hand picking olives. Cup thumb and index finger around the branch and pull downward. The olives will drop into the collecting bowl and the leaves will remain on the branch.

Picture: **H.**

Aleesha has picked some green olives that are now ready to be rinsed for the first step in processing.

Picture: **I.**

Olives that have been placed in a large plastic food safe colorless tub and gently rinsed with cold water. Any leaves, bad olives, sticks and other debris is removed. Be careful not to roughly bang olives together causing them to bruise.

Picture: **J.**

The rinsed olives are transferred to a two gallon glass jar. A small amount of water was poured into the bottom of the jar so the olives do not bruise when dropped into the jar.

Picture: **J2**.

The rinsed olives being gently placed into a two gallon jar. When the jar is full of olives, the lye solution will be added. Note: In this case a laundry sink has been placed outdoors for the processing procedures.

Picture: **J3.**

In this season an outdoor laundry sink was purchased and placed out on a covered patio. You can use your regular indoor laundry sink as long as it is thoroughly washed and is an area that is clean and sanitary. The rinsed olives are being gently placed in the two gallon glass Ball jar. The lye will be mixed with water and poured in to cover the olives.

Picture: **J4.**

If you cannot find two gallon Ball jars, you can find large glass or food/lye safe inert plastic jars at super (wholesale) food stores. I love large pickles. Just pour them into a zip lock bag and you have a big jar for your olive processing. This is a **one gallon glass** jar with large pickles from a warehouse/superstore. I always use glass jars and I recommend you do too. Also, Anchor Hocking makes a two and half gallon "glass barrow" jar.

Picture: **K.**

 Use a steel metal wire mesh "shaped" cover over the mouth of the jar to pour off the liquids. This wire cover can be used when pouring off lye/water and rinse/water. This is used so olives do not escape when draining the jar.

Picture: **L.**

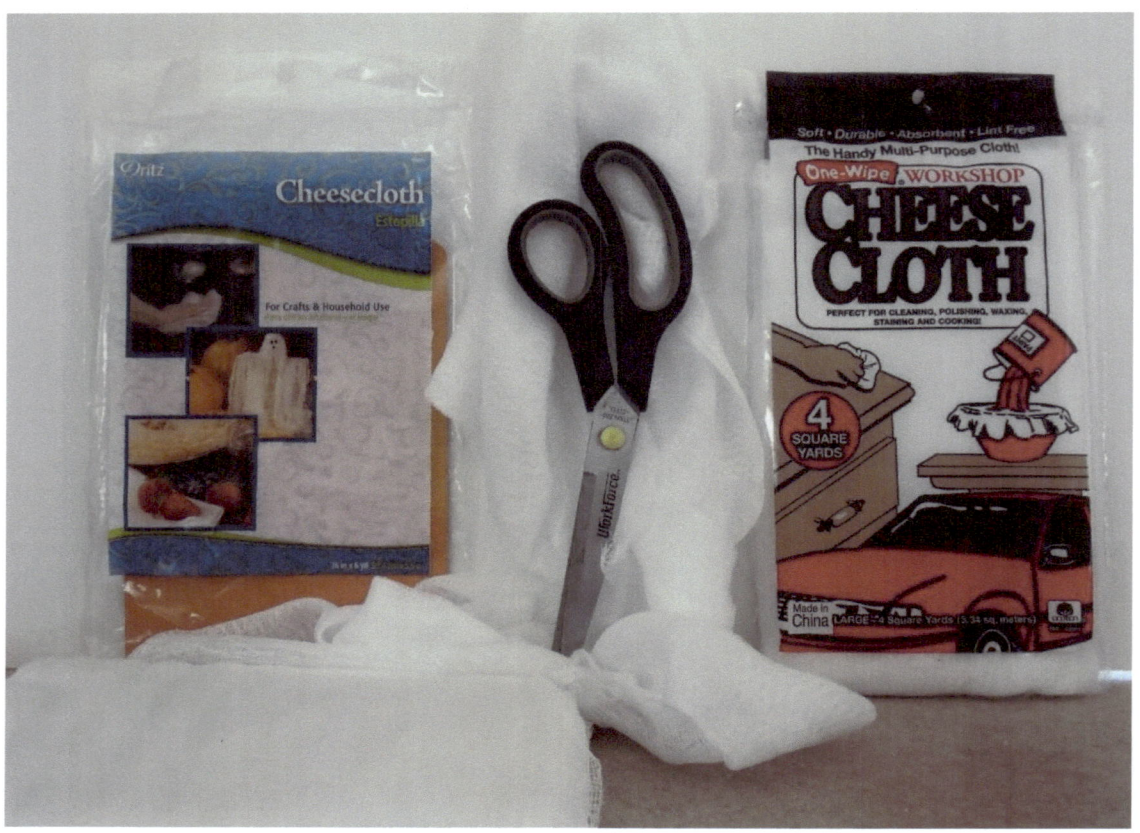

Cotton cheese cloth is used to top off jars during the lye and the rinsing procedures to keep air from contact with olives. Contact with air will discolor the olives. Contact with the air will **ruin** the olives by discoloring them.

Picture: **M.**

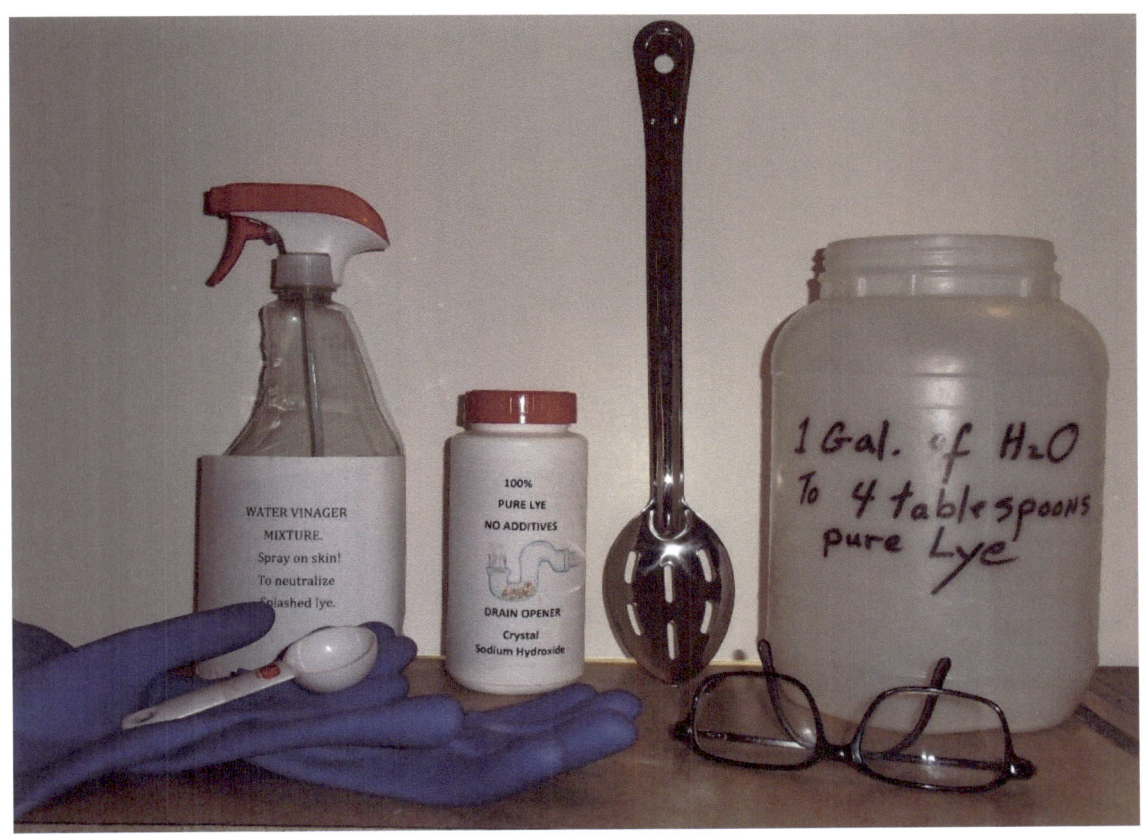

When the olives have been placed into two gallon glass jars. The jars are placed in a deep sink (laundry sink). The lye solution is ready to be mixed. Items needed are: 1. a measuring "table" spoon, metal (stainless steel) stirring spoon, rubber gloves, lye safe, inert, colorless plastic one gallon jar and pure lye. Remember your eye protection! Use only 100% pure lye (sodium hydroxide). If you are using drain cleaner, make sure it says 100% lye as above. If it does not, **do not use it**. Always slowly stir while adding lye to water, never add water to lye. It could act violently.

Picture: **N.**

Olives have been placed into two gallon glass jars. The lye solution has been added to about an inch and ½ from the top of the jar. A wad of cheese cloth is added to the top of the jar. Make sure the cheese cloth is pressed down tightly against the olives to eliminate air bubbles as you pour in more lye solution, saturating the cheese cloth to the very top of the jar. Cover the jar with plastic food wrap and the glass lids.

Picture: **O.**

Olives in two gallon glass jars. Lye solution has been added to the very tops of the jars. Under the glass lids are wads of cheese cloth to keep the olives at the top of the jars submerged in the solution so air cannot discolor them.

Picture: **O2.**

Laundry sink outside, food safe water hose, 2 gallon Ball jars with olives, cotton cheese cloth, plastic food wrap over mouth of jar, with cover. Picture taken during third day of cold water rinse cycle. Small jar between two gallon jars is a half-gallon jar with more olives.

Picture: **P.**

Quart jars being readied for the cured olives.

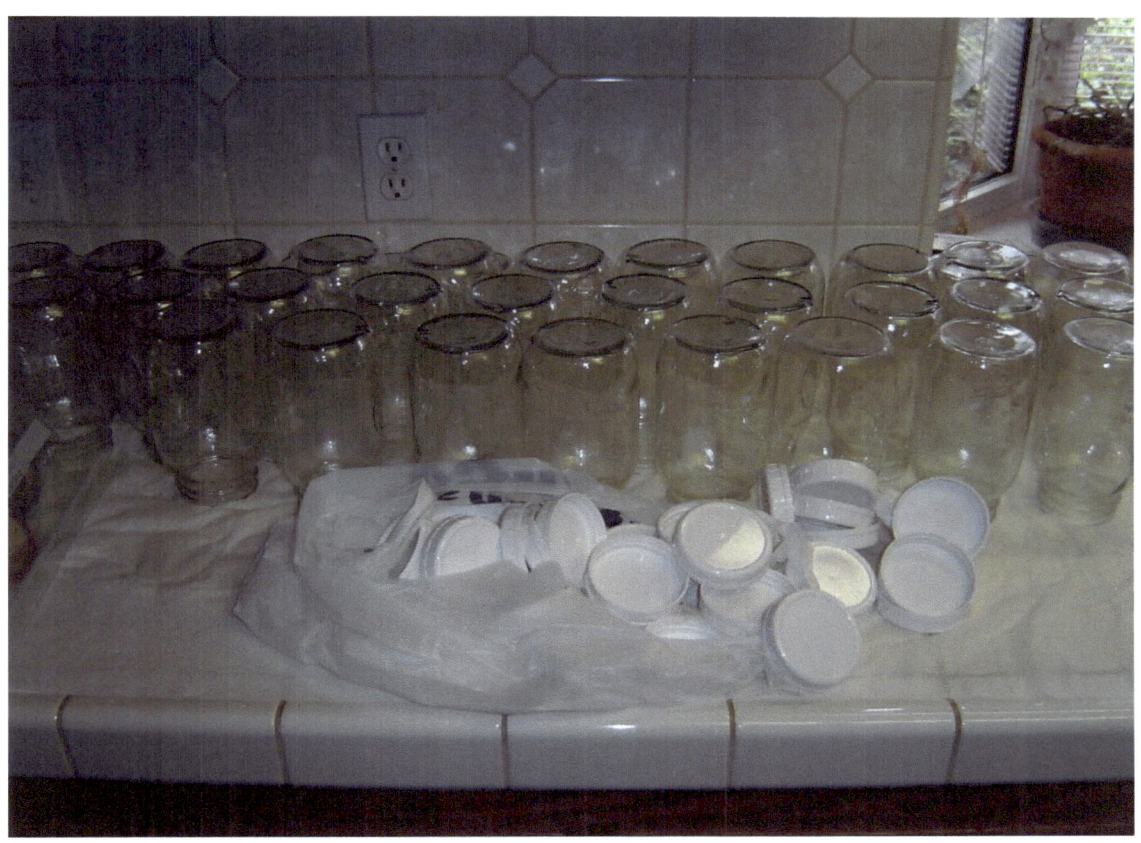

All the quart jars and lids need to be washed with warm soapy water and thoroughly rinsed and dried. You can use the metal canning lids or replace them with plastic (inert) mason jar lids as above. Jars should be labeled "refrigerate" or " - must refrigerate", indicating the olives were not " canning preserved".

Examples of Ingredients to be added to quart jars of olives.
I use these quality brands in my "Famous Fecher Pickled Olives".

Picture: **R3.**

Chopped up vegetables ready for olive jars.

Picture: **S.**

Quart jars are prepared to receive olives. Two inches of water/vinegar solution is added to each jar (Picture **S2**). Then the dry ingredients are added to the solution before the olives and vegetables are added.

Picture: **S2.**

Plastic food safe pitcher which has been filled with **one** part vinegar and **three** parts cold water.(More vinegar may be used but **not** less vinegar). Plastic food safe colorless basin is filled with washed olives ready to be put into quart jars with other ingredients to create "Famous Fecher Pickled Olives".

Picture: **T2.**

Famous Fecher Pickled Olives.

Finished olives with added condiments in their air tight quart jars (or pint jars) ready to be refrigerated. I refrigerate the olive jars from the beginning and recommend keeping them that way. (See label below).

MANZANILLO
PICKLED OLIVES
WITH PITS LEFT IN
Keep refrigerated
Shake well
Packed 11/2013

Epilog

About the Author.

In this closing section are items of the Author and the Authors past.

                                        Thank you,
                                        John

My friend: Budlite the cat (1998 -2013 R.I.P.)

Ode to Billy M.

I had a toy....a rag doll clown.
Smelled of perfume,
Squeezed and twisted, sawdust bones ground
And made a painful grinding sound.

But it still smiled....why do you frown?
I picked it up and threw it hard to the floor.
It lay there smiling and begged for more.
Kicked it then, an arm tore off.... A button eye was lost....
I was amused....
Perfume scent so strong it made me sneeze!

That was in my past when I was small
And have but vague memories to recall.
Now in my eyes the world goes round,
Humans bent down....
But not kicked by a foot
But by small words said or joking actions mocked....
To please one's own greedy lusts...

Bleed their guts, lick their wounds,
Musing, Crying, Hidden sounds.
But why do you frown?
There are so many.... Human Clowns.

I composed this poem for my cousin Billy in or about 1965. I received a letter from my mother that told me Billy had been drafted into the US Army and while at boot camp, in the northwest, he put a gun to his head and pulled the trigger. This poem came to me while on station in the Gulf of Tonkin. I was on watch in the after torpedo room of the submarine "USS Tang". Billy was my only male cousin. He was a few years older than me, he had an effeminate personality, not something the Army wanted in the 1960s. The perfume clown doll was given to me when I was 4 years old and sick in bed with the flu by my Aunty Jo, to cheer me up.

Oil on canvas from 1968.

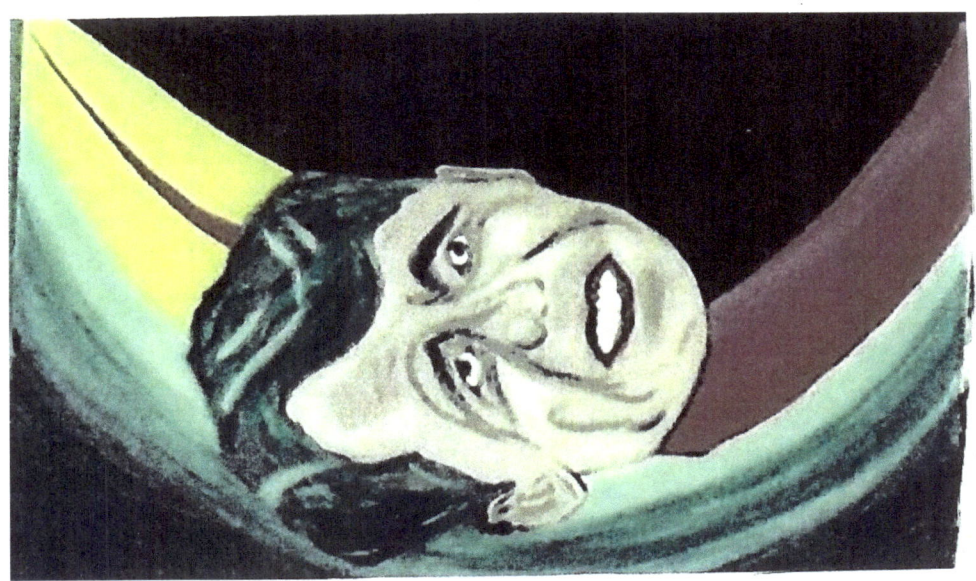

Top picture: Bobby Kennedy - Bottom: Vietnams Madonna & child.

Picture taken in Mid 1950s, Bay Shore, L.I., N.Y.

Gwen   Phyllis   Donna
1st girlfriend   sister   neighbor

Picture: Viola.

property of John E. Fecher   Photographer unknown

My mother, Viola, in her third grade "1922" class. She is the girl in the lower right corner of the picture. She and all the other children in this picture, taken that November day at school, have lived their lives, fulfilled their dreams?, been productive - or not, and are most likely now past on.

You're born, you live your life and die…now get on with living!

Picture: "Discouraged".

Pencil & pastels on paper – 1997.

Depicts the crew of the "U.S.S. Pueblo", Oil on canvas.
(24"X36") painted 1968.

Painting was left with a friend when I traveled that year. He stored it in his garage. His wife cleaned out the garage one day and the painting went to the dump. Faces are painted from shipmate photos from USS Blackfin, Tang and Tiru. Also Pres. Johnson, the Kennedys, Bob Dylan and me (at the nose of Johnson).

Charlie the dog was a good dog, 1999 – 2013.

Hi,

I hope you successfully cured olives using this book. If the olives were from your own trees, you may want to make it a yearly, family tradition. Your olives won't just fall to the ground and go to waste anymore.

I intend to donate the net profits and royalties from the sale of this book, annually, to local food banks and charities that feed people.

Yours Truly,

John

My H.S. Graduation.
(Property of John E. Fecher).

Me   Aunty Jo   Billy M.